Frack War:

THE NORTH FORK STRIKES BACK

ESSAY BY EVELYN SEARLE HESS

Frack War:

THE NORTH FORK STRIKES BACK

Graphic design by Andrew Sternard

ISBN for Paperback: 978-0-692-14979-9

Printed in the United States on sustainably certified paper.

Published 2018 by Citizens for a Healthy Community
Paonia, CO 81428

DEDICATION

———

To a courageous community, standing firm
with passion and ingenuity to protect its valley home.

———

ACKNOWLEDGEMENTS

—

So many people helped me through the twisted, bumpy, and sometimes backtracking path of the fight to preserve the North Fork Valley. I am deeply grateful to Wink Davis, Shirley Ela, Daniel Feldman, Brent Helleckson, Pete Kolbenschlag, Bob Lario, Natasha Léger, Jim Ramey, Sarah Sauter, Robin Smith, Tom Stevens, Kyle Tisdel, Mark Waltermire and anyone else I may have inadvertently neglected. I admire the sincerity, the work ethic, the respect for the earth and for one another of all these people, plus those I only read or was told about. Clean air, water, food and each other *must* prevail over exploitation and profit. Thank you for caring and staying strong.

—

DISCLAIMER

This essay is the result of individual interviews and secondary research conducted by the author. To the author's knowledge, the facts are accurate based on her research at the time of writing. The author sought to bring a human dimension to this story in focusing on the personalities of key actors. The views and opinions presented are solely those of the author.

Picture the most idyllic valley you can imagine. See it surrounded by mountains abounding with wildlife; clear, burbling streams with leaping fish; bald eagles perched atop old snags. You can hear kinglets as they sing and glean lunch in the mockorange, Black-Throated Warblers in the aspen and Meadowlarks on fence posts, as flycatchers swoop above the water to nab aerial insects. For well over a century, orchardists, vintners and organic farmers have sought out the valley below for its fertile soil, its climate, its clean air and water, and they continue to do so. Tourists meander, eager to sip fine wines or bite into a sweet and juicy peach as artists lay out their palettes to paint *en plein air.*

Now imagine that the scene turns dark, you hear spine-chilling music in the distance. Lights flash; thunder rumbles ever nearer; a swirling mist turns fetid. You're shaken with a foreboding of danger to the mountains and valley, to life and livelihood of all who live there now and in the future. How do you stand present in this beauty with the knowledge that it could all disappear? The thought makes your head buzz, your gut clench. You are living in a dream. How do you avoid waking up in a nightmare?

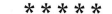

Shirley Ela (then Shirley Philips) may have bonded with the orchard in her infancy as she gazed at leaf patterns and shadows, listened to breezes and smelled the freshly irrigated soil, all from her mini-playpen—a fruit box plopped beneath the trees—under the watchful eye of a hired hand. Ninety years later, the orchard is still her favorite place, this perfect spot of western Colorado, between the mountains and the desert.

Shirley is a third-generation orchardist. In 1906, as land began to open up and pioneers dreamed of new lives, her grandparents, Frank and Maggie Burns, packed their belongings, loaded their animals into a railroad car, and moved their family from Iowa to the west slope of Colorado's Rocky Mountains, near Grand Junction. Frank planted peaches and lined irrigation ditches with boards to direct water to his trees and prevent erosion. His trees bore well when spring weather didn't freeze the flowers, and customers greeted the juicy fruit eagerly. Off-season or in bad years, he hauled gravel and lumber with his horse team to make ends meet. In the good years, any peaches they couldn't sell, the Burns dried on their roofs. Frank's mother would come west from Iowa to help with the harvest and the drying, and go back home with a winter's worth of dried fruit.

Frank and Maggie's daughter Lois married Nelson Newton Phillips in 1918. They bought land and planted pears, then apples and peaches. Shirley was their third child, but the first whose nursery was a box in the orchard. Her childhood memories revolve around the orchardist's life: those beautiful trees, the horse team pulling the wagon, with space left between boxes of fruit for a little girl to ride along; trekking across fourteen acres to deliver drinks to the packers by the time she was ten; joining her father on marketing trips and listening to his stories. One of those stories was inspired by the coddling moth. This creature, a constant challenge for apple growers, lays eggs that hatch as worms inside the apples. Philips said he graded his apples as clean, one-worm and two-worm. He gave the wry guarantee that if a customer bought a one-worm apple and it was clean, the buyer could trade it in for one with a worm in it.

The orchard's packing shed gave Shirley a job from the time she was a high-school freshman. Then to Junior College, where wartime training prepared her for a stint at Boeing Engineering in Seattle, marking corrections in plans for the B-17 planes. After Boeing, it was back to Boulder for a degree in sociology from the University of Colorado. Near her graduation, her high-school friend Bill Ela returned from the war, and "he looked pretty good in that uniform," Shirley remembers. They married and moved to Cambridge, Mass., where he would get his law degree at Harvard.

But the couple agreed that the West was the place to raise a family, and, Bill says, "I didn't just marry a wife. I married an orchard." They bought a farm adjoining the Philips' land and Bill practiced law and became a judge in western Colorado. With her father's help and tutelage, Shirley ran the tractor, the irrigation, the packing shed and the farm. By the late 1970s, development began to overrun their land near Grand Junction, surrounding it with subdivisions, roads, traffic and noise, so in the '80s, the Elas bought orchard property sixty miles southeast near Hotchkiss on Rogers Mesa, in the North Fork Valley of the Gunnison River and Shirley continued farming. Topping off her long career, in 2011 she was honored with a Lifetime Achievement Award from the Western Slope Horticultural Society.

With his academic background in biology, environmental geology, soil science and sustainable agriculture, Shirley and Bill's youngest son Steve now runs the farm, and Shirley and Bill have built a new house, bigger than a fruit box, in the middle of the orchard. That is where they plan to live out their lives. That also is where Steve, newly elected to the National Organic Standards Board, plans to continue farming in the valley's good soil. How many more generations of Elas will, from infancy, smell the clean spring air, hear and taste the mountain's pure water and listen to the songs of birds in the orchard?

Hotchkiss, population 944, Crawford, 431 and Paonia,

1451, (2011 numbers) nestle among organic farms, orchards, ranches and vineyards in the North Fork Valley, surrounded by mesas and mountain ridges. Mostly in public ownership—wilderness areas, national parks and BLM land—lakes and streams charged by snow in high mesas cut through near-vertical canyons, producing lush flora and fauna in surprising diversity for a high-desert environment. Sparkling creeks are home to brown, rainbow and brook trout.

Critical breeding, migration, and over-wintering habitat for numerous raptors, including Golden and Bald Eagles, American Kestral, Sharp-shinned, Cooper's, and Swainson's Hawks; Northern Goshawks, Peregrine and Prairie Falcons and Northern Harriers soar and nest in the valley. Ferruginous and Rough-legged Hawks, both species of concern, also cruise the skies. Side canyons echo with the music of songbirds including warblers, a group that gets along poorly with development and is therefore diminishing in number across the nation. The mountains invite camping, hunting, fishing, hiking, wildlife spotting, and species counting, as the valley lures farmers, ranchers, artists and tourists.

SAM WADE and **ENOS HOTCHKISS** were among the first European Americans to discover this hidden paradise. On their trek from the Midwest in the early 1880s, they marveled at the mild climate, water coursing down the canyon sides that could be made available for irrigation, rich bottomland soils and the protection afforded by the mountains and mesas. Healthy native fruiting plants such as hawthorne, chokecherry and buffaloberry gave Wade hope that the land would support domestic fruits as well. In the spring following his return to Missouri, he brought back 200 apple trees, ten each pear and apricot trees, twenty sapling peaches, 200 cherry trees, 100 grape vines, 1000 blackberries, 100 raspberries, twelve currants and fifty gooseberries, planting them on his farm, which would later become the town of Paonia. Though he lost a third of his plants the first winter, the rich alluvial soil produced even healthier plants than he had expected. Having begun with those orchards, the valley now supplies 77% of Colorado's apples and 71% of the state's peaches. Wade also brought in a load of his favorite flower, the peony. The Post Office thought there were too many vowels in peony's botanical name, *Paeonia*, but it was those flowers that gave the town of Paonia its name, shortchanged by one vowel.

At about the same time that Sam Wade was planting orchards and building irrigation ditches in what would become Paonia, and Enos Hotchkiss was putting in his own fruit trees about nine miles southwest in what would become his namesake town of Hotchkiss, geologists discovered coal about ten miles northeast of Paonia. Though begun modestly, mines became an economic driver for the area. By 1902, a railroad ran from the mines through Paonia and Hotchkiss, hauling not only coal, but also fruit, making a name for the valley, and providing means for the whole state to taste the prize-winning produce of those early orchards.

As **STEVE ELA,** the fourth generation orchardist at Ela Family Farms, began to transition to organic growing, others were discovering this high fertile valley along the North Fork of the Gunnison River. **EAMES PETERSEN** learned winemaking in Spain and brought the old methods back to the States. He planted a vineyard near Paonia in 1994 and by 2012 his Alfred Eames Cellar label was already outshining French wines at juried tastings. **BRENT HELLECKSON** also chose the Paonia end of the North Fork Valley to establish his Stone Cottage Wine Cellars, after he left his Boulder career as an aerospace engineer in 1994. Helleckson and his wife Karen dug foot-wide and bigger stones from the soil as they prepared to plant their vineyards. They used those stones to build their vineyard's namesake cottage and, later, a half-buried wine cellar, a tasting room and eventually, their own home. Buildings, vineyard, harvesting, winemaking and bottling, all are family projects. The Hellecksons moved to the North Fork Valley to live close to the land and raise their family sustainably. It's the lifestyle they were seeking.

Stone Cottage Cellars and their neighbor Terror Creek Winery both sit high above the valley. At over six thousand feet elevation, they boast astonishing views of the valley below and the snow-covered mountain ridges beyond as well as unique climate for the production of fine wine. Now with eleven wineries making wine from some of the highest vineyards in the northern hemisphere, the North Fork Valley's West Elks is one of only two American Viticultural Areas (AVAs) in Colorado. To qualify as an AVA, vineyards must lie in a limited region with distinguishable characteristics such as soil, elevation and climate. Surrounded on three sides by mountain ranges and mesas and on the fourth by desert badlands, the area is clearly delimited. Three hundred sunny days a year fill the fruits with sugar; cool nights capture acidity; rich but well-drained soils make for unique crisp and flavorful wines, gaining the West Elks AVA justifiable fame.

MARK WALTERMIRE, one of several organic farmers in the area, came to the North Fork Valley with degrees in biology and environmental studies, plus years of agricultural and teaching experience in Pakistan, California, Montana and Massachusetts. In 2005, with his wife **KATIE DEAN** and their two young sons, he set up his sixteen-acre Thistle Whistle Farm, where he produces 200 varieties of heirloom and specialty vegetables and easily sells all he grows. Dedicated to empowering others to live well, Mark runs an apprenticeship program on his farm, training future sustainable farmers. The interns learn as they work, as well as in classes and by taking part in on-site trials, such as one exploring mycorrhizal effects on fruit trees. Waltermire provides his interns lodging, plenty of fresh produce, information, a small stipend and the keys to a fulfilling future. Besides supplying interesting, tasty and healthful food to the public and mentoring budding organic growers, Mark inspires with community classes and hosts school field trips, The Sauce Plot Kids Camp, and English as a Second Language for Nutrition.

In 2008, after twenty years in the restaurant business and a year studying cheese-making in the United Kingdom, **WENDY MITCHELL** began the Avalanche Cheese Company in Basalt, CO, near Aspen. Then realizing no reliable source existed for the volume of milk she needed, she began a 130-acre goat dairy farm in Paonia, "the heart of Colorado's Farm to Table movement." As she had learned cheese making, she now had to learn goat farming, and was gratified the valley's farmers were willing to tutor and support this "city girl." Her goat cheeses quickly got contracts with Whole Foods and with dozens of Aspen- and Paonia-area high-end restaurants and shops. Mitchell's cheese company regularly sells out at the Aspen Saturday Market.

With the productivity and natural beauty of the valley, its mountains and waterways seducing visitors to fishing, hiking and watersports, and now with the burgeoning food and wine industries, the North Fork Valley has become a major tourist attraction. **MARLEY HODGSON** sold his New York City leather goods business in 2000 to re-build, log by log, and renovate existing ranch buildings, some that had been built high above the village of Crawford in the late 1800s, with others added from the 1920s to '50s. While honoring that history, Hodgson and his wife **LINDA** established an upscale dude ranch. At $6,200 a week for a couple of guests, and a seasonal staff of thirty-five, their Smith Fork Ranch uses locally-grown produce and adds about a million dollars a year to the economy.

As the valley becomes better known, retired people seeking an active life without the intensity often found in high-end retirement communities, discover its unspoiled beauty. Artists and other professionals who work remotely find their ideal nests as well. The valley now is rich in studios and workshops of traditional artists: weavers, blacksmiths, carvers, quilters; fine artists: potters, painters, photographers and sculptors; writers, performing artists, tech artists, culinary artists and creators of value-added products. In 2012, the North Fork Valley was named an "Emerging Creative District" by Colorado Creative Industries, a division of the Governor's Office of Economic Developments and International Trade. In June of 2013, that designation was boosted to Certified Creative District status.

TOM STEVENS searched for the perfect place before he moved to the North Fork Valley. For twenty years a realtor in Boulder, he was frustrated by the changes brought by extractive energy industries there. The moment he decided to move may have come as he advised a friend of the worth of her farm. She had come to him in frustration. Many people don't realize that they can own their home, their orchard, their ranch, but have legal rights only from the ground up. When the west was opened for expansion, the government often retained control of any minerals below the ground even when people assumed their property was truly theirs. Not having the mineral rights to her land, Stevens' friend was now surrounded by 16 oil wells, one less than twenty feet from her house. "I can't stand it any more," she said. "The noise, the smell, the dirt, trucks running back and forth... I can't use my land. I have no peace. I have to get out."

"And I had to tell her," Stevens said, "You won't be able to sell your land now. It is virtually worthless."

So Stevens went searching for an undamaged place where people could live an authentic life with trust in the future, and he found the North Fork Valley. On the edge of the town of Crawford, he found green meadows near an imposing boulder called Needle Rock, a branch of the valley disappearing into a narrow opening in the bordering hills. He imagined horses grazing, deer leaping over fences, the ideal siting for a house and barn.

Stevens finally began to relax, shrugging off what had become an omnipresent shadow of impending doom, and dared once again to dream. He signed the contract for this perfect spread.

Alfred Eames' son was absorbing the secrets of fine wine in order to become his father's heir apparent; Mark Waltermire welcomed new interns eager to learn how to farm sustainably; Steve Ela's customers exclaimed over his "O-mi-god-delicious" organic peaches and the ink was barely dry on Tom Stevens' commitment to the land when he and the rest of the valley awoke one blustery December day of 2011 to staggering news:

THE BLM WAS ANNOUNCING THE LEASE SALE OF 33,000 NORTH FORK VALLEY ACRES FOR OIL AND GAS DRILLING.

Historically, people had understood that the Mancos shale underlying the North Fork Valley—the very shale giving the soil above its water-holding capacity and unique flavoring attributes so appreciated by local farmers and their customers—was not conducive to drilling. Any oil or gas that might be in or under the rock would be next to impossible to get to, using conventional extraction methods. But that was before hydraulic fracturing (fracking) came on the scene. In this process, and with the horizontal drilling and multi-stage system expected to be required for Mancos shale, two to eight million gallons of water, sand and chemicals under pressures sometimes exceeding 9000 pounds per square inch are injected down one to two miles below the surface and then horizontally a mile or more, literally fracturing the earth's bones. Sand particles hold the cracks open so that the natural gas or oil can be pumped up the well. Since 2005, 18,168 wells have been drilled in Colorado, with nearly 2000 in 2012 alone, each well directly impacting about nine acres of land, and with that, introducing concerns about water pollution, water scarcity, air pollution, dust and noise, roaring trucks and hundreds of miles of new roads.

Was the pristine North Fork Valley, home to Colorado's largest concentration of organic farms, to become just another industrial area?

Not if we have anything to say about it,

respond Valley residents. **ROBIN SMITH** and **DANIEL FELDMAN** had come to the valley with their respective families a mere two years before the BLM announcement. Robin and his wife, **CYNTHIA WUTCHIETT,** had worked hard and lived frugally in Columbus, Ohio, squirreling away whatever they could spare, driven by the vision of leaving the hurry-scurry world of credit cards, sirens and screeching brakes for an early retirement to simple and sustainable lives. When they discovered the North Fork Valley, they knew they had found their paradise.

Daniel and **JOANN FELDMAN** studied permaculture and sustainable agriculture while they searched the western Rockies for the right spot to realize their vision of responsible and self-sufficient farming. They too found the North Fork Valley. But even as the last bricks were being laid on the Smith and Feldman dream homes, they heard rumors of gas development at the headwaters of the Gunnison River.

Feeling the need to have strong and cohesive public protection for a place of such exceptional natural diversity and creative productivity, Joann Feldman and others began organizing concerned locals into a nucleus that would become Citizens for a Healthy Community (CHC). Robin Smith made contact with the Western Environmental Law Center (WELC) in Taos to be sure legal help would be available if needed. Their concerns didn't develop at that time, but now the stakes were much higher and CHC begins to mobilize.

SARAH SAUTER had arrived in Paonia just a year earlier as the new Executive Director of The Conservation Center. This thirty-five-year old non-profit environmental group has a diverse mission, working with water issues, education, recycling, "to build an active and aware community to protect and enhance the lands, air, water and wildlife of the Lower Gunnison Watershed." The BLM's announcement threatened an assault on many fronts, and posed serious endangerment to watercourses and ecosystems. Clearly, it was time to involve the public. Her thick blonde braid swinging, Sarah Sauter shifted into high gear.

Smith and Feldman were grateful for having the WELC legal team on their side, but they needed maximum involvement from the community as well. So together, CHC and Sarah Sauter's TCC put up a Facebook page called North Fork Fracking, with bright red lines surrounding potential oil leases on maps of the area. The BLM's proposed wells could endanger the valley's drinking and irrigation water, jeopardize mountains and streams used for recreation, compromise habitat for elk and other wildlife, threaten countless livelihoods and destroy the character of the valley. The two organizations sent out flyers, public service announcements, radio and newspaper releases, phone calls and emails, informing the public, encouraging them to pass the word about the threat and its possible ramifications.

What would happen to the wine makers, the fruit growers, the artists and the tourist businesses? What would happen to Thistle Whistle Farm and Ela Family Farms and all of the organic farming customers and students?

Property desirability and values would also be seriously affected. Realtor **BOB LARIO** came to the North Fork Valley in 1970 by way of a New Jersey ghetto, where he had taught science, and California, where he had migrated from the east coast along with others of the "Back-to-the-Earth" movement. In 1976, he and his wife **LINDA** began their now life-long career as realtors. In an area like this, he says, "there are rewards other than money." People come to the North Fork Valley, Lario has found, because of the quality of life here. Their livelihoods may be *enhanced* by the purity of the water and the health of the soil or it may actually *depend* on them. They may already have financed their lives, or be able to conduct business online or they may need peaceful surroundings to inspire their music or art. But the unique clean quiet safe beauty of the valley is non-negotiable. With even a hint that drilling might begin, numbers of potential real estate buyers plunge. Even some sales-in-progress decide to pull out. What would happen to the real estate market, and the realtors? What would happen to the hikers and campers, the fishers and hunters? What would happen to the animals whose habitats or migration routes were disrupted, or those who require undeveloped land?

As Citizens for a Healthy Community and The Conservation Center scrambled to contact, inform and energize the community, a man with curly graying hair and short-cropped beard appeared in Sarah's office. His eyes sparkled with stored energy and a hint of a private joke that belied his quiet but intense demeanor. This was **PETE KOLBENSCHLAG,** a member of Colorado's Environmental Coalition and owner of Mountain West Strategies. Long active at the state level, he had maintained a low profile locally, so, though Sarah welcomed his help, she didn't initially realize the resource and talent she was getting. It turned out that Pete was not only a top-notch organizer throughout and beyond Colorado, he also had deep experience with and knowledge of the workings of the BLM.

In spite of those BLM connections though, the oil and gas lease-sale plans caught Pete, like everyone else, by complete surprise. When he first heard the news, he put a map on the wall with a bright blue pin marking his property, then plotted out the proposed leases. They were on all sides. He was surrounded: a noose around his neck.

Pete had been going through a hard time in his personal life and now as he stared at the map, he could feel "the third shoe about to drop." Riveted to the image on the wall, anger welled up. "No!" he thought. "I'm not going to let this happen!" He took a few deep breaths, set his jaw, and went to join CHC and the Conservation Center.

Over in Crawford, Tom Stevens looked over his meadows, focusing on his imagined future and had similar thoughts. *Such a pristine place here. No way can I face watching my world destroyed again. I can't run. I've got to stop it.*

January 4, 2012, more than five hundred locals gather at the Paonia Junior High School gym. Maps taped to the walls show the locations of the proposed drilling parcels. Tension fills the room, occasional voices exploding over the background buzz.

Can you believe this? This one is right by the school!

Here's one by the reservoir!

Oh God! Two are practically in my backyard. And three more in my view of the mountains!

Farmers, doctors, ranchers, artists; all professions, all ages, crowd onto the gym bleachers and pack the chairs set up on the court. Dozens more shoulder into standing room in the back. Residents are anxious, confused, angry, determined.

Panelists give an overview of the situation. Tension builds; agitated voices rumble. A panelist mentions that it takes 1,000 to 1,500 truck trips—huge trucks—to develop each well, reminding people of the noise, dust, congestion and road-wear that would produce. Someone points out that each gas well requires up to eight million gallons of water. *We've been forced to scrimp on water already!* someone else exclaims, as recent droughts have made farms, orchards and ranches struggle to find enough to get by.

CHC chairman Daniel Feldman shares with the public what the organizing groups have found particularly infuriating: the resource management plan on which the BLM is basing its leasing parcels was adopted in 1989. "Over two decades ago! Most of the organic farms and wineries, as well as some of the schools weren't even here when it was written. The valley has changed since 1989, and the BLM needs to know that. At the very least, they should be working from a current plan."

Then Sarah Sauter's Americorp-Vista volunteer presents the *tour de force* of the evening, a virtual flyover of the area, using GoogleEarth mapping. As neighbors in the jam-packed gymnasium "fly" over their valley, seeing the reality of wells in their watershed, their viewshed, their and their children's lives, it is as if five hundred people have gone mute, total silence broken only by an occasional gasp or sob. Lease parcels completely surround the valley.

KYLE TISDEL, the environmental attorney from Taos, looks out at the crowd, gratified at their engagement and determined to do everything in his power to support them. It was for moments exactly like this that he had felt called to public interest service: using the power of the law to support the needs of the people. Money had never been a motivator. The people's number-one need is protection of the environment, and climate change, the environment's gravest threat, is inseparable from development and use of fossil fuels and energy.

Tisdel explains the legal framework for challenging the BLM if they won't respond to citizen complaints, and says it is WELC's goal to assure that critical areas are permanently protected and that no shale gas development happens without environmental safeguards to protect both human and wildlife communities. Someone in the crowd shouts, "Who is it that wants to drill? If there's digging going on in my back yard, I ought to know who's holding the shovel."

BLM policy is to keep the identity of the nominators confidential, Tisdel says. "But we agree with you. You should know," and goes on to tell the crowd that WELC will be filing a Freedom of Information Act request to find out exactly that. All federal agencies must comply with FOIA. There are exemptions to the type of information that can be disclosed, but they should not be a problem for this case.

Heads seem to be held higher throughout the gymnasium, as the promise of legal support steels a growing resolve to fight for what each person present, individually or as part of the community, loves.

For four hours, community members ask questions or contribute information and share their personal stories and concerns. Someone says, "I get that the BLM needs to provide for multiple uses and mineral extraction is a use. But how can it justify a use that will destroy other existing uses?"

Pete Kolbenschlag, speaking of huge parcels at the base of Mt Lamborn, the summit dominating the valley, points out that those parcels are on geologically unstable land and right under avalanche chutes.

Someone adds that fracking causes seismic activity, and wonders what that might do to coal miners working in underground tunnels.

Steve Ela tells the group that Ela Family Farms has put over a million dollars into the farm and they've been organically certified since 1995. He reminds folks that there are a lot of organic farms, grass-fed beef ranching and micro-cheeseries in the valley, all dependent on clear water and a clean environment. The organic label and the quality of Ela's apples and juicy peaches—like the produce from the several dozen other organic growers in the valley—would be in serious jeopardy with expected air or water pollution.

Then **THEO COLBORN,** now 84, takes the stand. To thundering applause and a standing ovation, her ever-ready smile, steely-gray cropped hair and wide eyes as bright and penetrating as they must have been at twenty, the revered local scientist looks out at her friends and neighbors. Her voice passionate, she lists harmful impacts on human health of shale-gas drilling's toxic by-products. These include brain, nervous system and immune system effects; endocrine disruptors; carcinogens; chemicals affecting the G.I. tract, the cardiovascular system, kidneys, liver and metabolic processes, plus several chemicals that are genotoxic. Nationally controversial but fearless, Dr. Colborn was among the first to bring an awareness of endocrine-disrupting effects of even very small doses of chemicals. As important as it had been for her to ferret out these effects, she now felt an urgency to share the information.

THEO COLBORN, born Theodora Emily Decker, March 28, 1927 in Plainfield, N.J., was honing her love for the out of doors at about the same time that Shirley Ela was bonding with her Colorado orchard from her nursery-box cradle. From her earliest childhood memories, Colborn was fascinated with birds, the natural world, river water and trying unsuccessfully to find answers to "why?" and "how?" By the time she hit high school, she revolted against prescriptions directing girls to courses that prepared them for secretarial or teaching careers, and opted instead for "boys only" classes in science. There, she exceled. On a visit with a high school counselor to the Rutgers University, she fell in love with everything she saw. However, practicality told her she couldn't afford to go to college at all, so she got a job as a laboratory technician right after graduation. Before long however, word came that Vicks Chemical Company had awarded her a four-year scholarship to Rutgers' College of Pharmacy.

After getting her Bachelor of Science degree, Theo married Harry Colborn, a WWII vet and fellow pharmacy student studying on the G.I. Bill. Together they had three pharmacies and four children, taking the family birding, camping and exploring the out-of-doors as often as possible. Looking for quieter and wilder lives, in the early 1960s the Colborns sold their pharmacies and headed west beyond the ridge of the Rocky Mountains. Thrilled with the rugged landscape and peaceful valley along the north fork of the Gunnison River, they bought land near Hotchkiss.

But before long, Theo became uncomfortable selling pharmaceuticals without patients understanding the drug's possible side effects. And at about the same time, she noticed ill health in locals who drank water from where coal mining had polluted the Gunnison River. She wanted good data to fight for the health of the people and the waterways, but couldn't find any. So she found a job sampling the Gunnison River and its tributaries.

In her early fifties, Theo went back to school, spending her summers doing field research at the Rocky Mountain Biological Laboratories in Crested Butte, studying the effects on aquatic life of pollutant residues from coal mining. In 1981, her Masters thesis, titled *Aquatic insects as measures of trace element presence: cadmium and molybdenum,* was accepted by Western State College of Colorado, in Gunnison, and at age 54, she had a Masters' degree in fresh-water ecology.

Theo wanted to learn more. So she began studies in zoology at the University of Wisconsin, Madison. At age 58, she was awarded a Ph.D. in zoology with distributed minors in epidemiology, toxicity and water chemistry. She then applied for and received a White House fellowship in the Office of Technology Assessment.

After her fellowship, Colborn worked with the newly merged World Wildlife Fund and Conservation Foundation, doing research on contaminants in the Great Lakes. Many scientists had worked there, but they had not compared data. At a time when most scientists were reductionists, Theo was a synthesizer. She gathered the literature and produced a spreadsheet with animal names on the "Y" axis and observed effects on the "X" axis. Resulting information was stunning. She found numerous species with reproductive and immune system problems and behavioral, hormonal and metabolic changes even when the toxin dose was well below that considered safe.

Whole populations were declining or disappearing; many species showed birth defects or wasting before or after hatching; scientists observed ineffective mating behavior, thyroid problems, fish and amphibians with both male and female organs. The worst effects were in the young or in the unborn fetus and embryo. Often an adult predator—avian, mammal or other—eating fish from the Great Lakes would show no effects, but their progeny, if successfully born or hatched, would have significant metabolic, neurological or behavioral problems and frequently would not live long enough to reproduce. One study reported that babies of human mothers eating Great Lakes fish two or three times per month had lower birth weight and had changes in their brains, visible on MRIs. In a paper explaining these effects, Colborn and others described how the toxic substances in the body block intercellular communication that would otherwise direct cellular migration and differentiation at early stages of development. These pollutants, even in very low doses, can affect bones, heart, nervous and reproductive systems.

The ultimate "knitter," as one colleague called her, "both of ideas and of people," and motivated by the Great Lakes experience, in 1990 Colborn convened 21 scientists from several disciplines to discuss environmental endocrine-disrupting chemicals and their effects. This work became part of the background for her 1996 book, *Our Stolen Future*, co-authored with Diane Dumanoski and Pete Myers. Written for the popular audience, this book has been compared to *Silent Spring*, both from its effectiveness alerting the public to a problem and for the violent and insulting reaction its authors received from Industry.

In 2003, at age 76, Theo returned to Paonia and founded The Endocrine Disruption Exchange (TEDX), an international nonprofit organization for the purpose of "compiling and disseminating scientific evidence on health and environmental problems caused by low-dose exposure to chemicals that interfere with development and function." Her staff continues her "big-picture" dedication to inter-disciplinary work and her passion for supporting women in science. It is composed of women with advanced degrees in cognitive science, endocrinology and reproduction, and integrative physiology. Now, besides looking at agricultural and industrial chemicals that have seeped or been dumped into waterways, Colborn and TEDX study environmental health effects of natural gas extraction, particularly those of fracking. The public isn't privy to the cocktails of chemicals injected while drilling, but of those that are known, many are toxic. This polluted water can come back to the surface or migrate underground to waterways or water-well sites.

A number of highly toxic gases besides methane are present at the wellhead, among them the "aromatics," collected in condensate tanks and delivered to chemical and product-manufacturing industries. These are the feedstock for much of what make our lives easier and more hazardous: the plastics and pesticides, cleaning products and fragrances, fire retardants, pharmaceuticals, toys and electronics whose off-gassing can enter the womb through the mother's placenta and cause endocrine-driven disorders like ADHD, autism, diabetes, obesity, endometriosis and early testicular cancer.

Theo Colborn says that the rest of her life is "dedicated to spreading the word that fossil fuels are not only linked to climate change, but also to the plethora of epidemics resulting from exposure to their end-use products." Looking to an uncertain future as they leave the meeting that wintry evening in 2012, the citizens of North Fork Valley are grateful to have Dr. Colborn in their corner.

* * * * *

After Dr. Colborn speaks, Feldman tells the crowd that

because of the flood of calls and emails the BLM has received, the comment period has been extended to February 9. "Go to the wall maps," he urges the audience, "Find every spot you care about—your homes, work, hiking or fishing places—and note every school, domestic well, irrigation ditch, or spring that could be damaged by drilling. Then write a letter to the BLM, being as specific as possible."

Though most of the people at the meeting are understandably focused on effects on their own businesses and ways of life, Dr. Colborn has given them a wider perspective—something else to think about as they write their letters to the BLM.

Fired up after the public meeting, the com-

munity gets busy. By February 9, the end of the extended comment period, they write and send over 3,000 letters, plus dozens of official protests and phone calls to the BLM. WELC files technical comments on behalf of CHC outlining legal deficiencies in the BLM's NEPA (National Environmental Policy Act) analysis for the lease sale as well as human health and climate risks of fracking. Citizens for a Healthy Community, until now strictly a volunteer organization, adds to its Board of Directors, and advertises for an Executive Director. Frustrated by learning that the BLM, though presumably generating a revised version, is still working from a 1989 Resource Management Plan, local citizens from business, agriculture, resource and conservation communities join forces to create their own alternative plan—one that will truly respect multiple uses, as the BLM claims to do, including those both of the environment and of the community.

Meanwhile, people get back to their lives. Orchardists and viticulturists have pruning to do; farmers prepare the soil for planting and check their irrigation canals and ditches; the town of Hotchkiss readies for the annual sheepdog trials; ranchers gather cattle for the spring drive through Crawford to lush higher pastures.

By Spring, CHC has found its Executive Director. **JIM RAMEY,** living in Montrose, fifty miles from Paonia with his attorney wife, Lindsey, brings a background in energy and degrees in political science from the University of Cincinnati and in Public Administration from Ohio State. Jim jumps feet first into the middle of the fray, just in time to learn that the BLM has denied WELC's Freedom of Information Act (FOIA) request for the names of the oil and gas lease nominators.

In Mid-April, as new leaf-buds on vines begin to break, Pete Kolbenschlag and a delegation from CHC head to Washington D.C. to talk to Colorado legislators and to the U.S. Director of the BLM. Legislators and agency heads in Washington need to understand what's happening locally—the potential risks to the health and wellbeing of the citizens, the wildlife and the economy.

On a sunny day in early May, as Sarah Sauter strides

down the street in Paonia, a woman she doesn't remember having met rushes up to her, throws her arms around Sarah and sobs, "We won! We won! Can you believe it? Thank you! Thank you! Thank you! I am so happy!!"

It is news to Sarah, but it's true. The BLM has deferred the leasing of all 22 parcels. Was it the trip to D.C.? The legal presence? The public outcry?" The North Fork Valley community is giddy. *We did it! We did it!* You can *too* fight city hall!—or in this case, a federal bureau. Some begin to relax. Some are hard at work on developing a community alternative for the resource management plan revision, already in the works. Some, though pleased for any delay, are all too aware that a deferral is not a cancellation. The area is still exploitable for the potential riches hiding deep within the ground. And in June, WELC files a federal case to force disclosure of the nominators' identities.

In November, the aspens still splashing gold

across snow-dusted hills, Valley citizens learn that the White River National Forest Service is drafting a 15-20-year oil and gas plan. If citizens can do their research and organize quickly, they now have a chance to weigh in.

Immediately north and east of the North Fork Valley, the 2.3-million-acre White River National Forest includes eight wilderness areas, with ten mountain peaks over 14,000 feet high. One edge of the forest brushes the top of Mt. Aspen. Throughout, it hosts cattle ranching, tourism, hiking, camping, hunting, fishing and skiing. Called by Gov. Hickenlooper the "crown jewel" of the area, the 220,000-acre Thompson Divide lies within both the White River and the Gunnison National Forests. It runs through parts of five counties and holds 81 mineral leases, covering nearly half of its total acreage. Just west of the Divide, oil and gas activity has turned tens of thousands leased acres in Gunnison County alone from wild lands to potential or active industrial expanse.

But now, before that work spreads farther, the public has an opportunity to give input to the planning process. Citizens are urged to tell the Forest Service, "No drilling in the Thompson Divide!" Locals are aghast and visitors incredulous that drilling could be considered in this rugged and flourishing landscape. Perhaps it wouldn't have come as such a surprise though, if the populace had been aware earlier of what had been going on in Washington D.C.

When George W. Bush left Texas and his oil interests for the White House, energy exploration was high on his agenda. With the encouragement of his administration, the BLM, which manages all federal minerals, including those in national forests, put millions of acres up for auction, often slighting both environmental analysis and public notification. The fervor of the moment encouraged what Peter Hart, a Wilderness Workshop attorney, called a "lease before you look" mentality.

During this period of furious speculation, the only way to find out about a proposed lease sale might be to stumble on a note tacked to a bulletin board. The plan for leasing in the Thompson Divide might not have been discovered before drilling was active but for the sharp eyes of an attorney in the public interest environmental law firm Earthjustice. He saw a notice of an upcoming auction and spotted proposed leases in a roadless area. Joining with Wilderness Workshop, he filed a challenge, alerting others to the potential threat.

As environmental watchdog groups prevailed in challenges to the Department of Interior's Board of Land Appeals, the Bush Administration worked on a new energy policy. Overseen by vice president Dick Cheney, former head of fracking-fluid-providing Halliburton Industries, and with major input from representatives of the oil and gas industry, the stated purpose of the 2005 Energy Act was to "ensure jobs for our future with secure, affordable and reliable energy." The act changed US energy policy by providing tax incentives and loan guarantees for energy production and exempting the industry from many public health and environmental laws. Thanks to the Act, oil and gas producers need no longer worry about the Clean Air or Clean Water Acts or the Safe Drinking-Water Act. The Energy Act creates a loophole exempting producers from disclosing the chemicals used in fracking, and it directs the Secretary of the Interior to analyze a program to lease shale and tar sands on public lands, particularly in Colorado, Utah and Wyoming.

And so the rush began, virtually unfettered, to explore, exploit and profit from the seductive geology of the Thompson Divide, among other places. Now residents from Aspen to Paonia, passionate to save the stunning Divide from transformation to oilfields, plunge into the fight.

Focused on soliciting and sending letters

to protect the Thompson Divide, CHC and residents of the North Fork Valley are blindsided when, in the middle of that same November, the BLM announces it is putting twenty parcels, about 20,000 acres of land in and around the valley, back on the auction block, scheduled for sale February, 2013. Once again the timing of the announcement, and therefore of the requisite 30-day protest deadline, coincides with the holiday season. Is that a coincidence? And with the FOIA request to reveal the nominators' identities denied by BLM, WELC is in the midst of briefing the still-pending subsequent federal court case. Frustrated, undoubtedly at least a little angry but ever more determined, CHC and WELC prepare a formal protest to Helen Hankins, Colorado's State Director of the BLM.

December 14, 2012, WELC sends a 36-page letter on behalf of CHC, protesting the environmental assessment and Finding of No Significant Impact (FONSI) reached by BLM's local Uncompahgre Field Office (UFO). The FONSI is particularly aggravating. After individuals, organizations and governmental agencies sent more than 3000 carefully researched letters enumerating the myriad ways that oil and gas development was incompatible with their lives and work, as well as with the health of wildlife and preservation of natural attributes, BLM's UFO issued a FONSI. "No significant impact" in the face of possible pollution of air, water and soil, endangering human health as well as the certification of organic farms, orchards and vineyards and the quality of their products? "No Significant Impact" though drilling would disrupt breeding and migrating grounds of wildlife, clearly impacting fishing and hunting in addition to the wildlife itself? "No Significant Impact" in the potential destruction of the tourist business and property values? Not, of course, to mention "No Significant Impact" to climate change. Farmers, ranchers, realtors and outdoorsmen and women would dispute the insignificance of those effects.

The Protest goes on to point out that the BLM's environmental analysis had little in common with the one they made public the previous spring, but in spite of that, allows no public comment. One area that does remain the same is the peculiar claim that no analysis is required before leasing and companies apply for permits to drill. The coy rationale given is that no impacts would accrue from the mere leasing of parcels, ignoring the fact that once a lease is purchased, the lessee has the right to use the land as deemed necessary for exploration and exploitation. The WELC letter insists that potential problems must be identified and avoided. They must not be ignored, with the hope of being corrected after the fact.

The WELC protest reminds the government, the community and the public that the BLM is still working from its 1989 resource management plan, the plan that delineates how mineral-resource decisions are to be made. Not only does the old Resource Management Plan not reflect current conditions and development, but any lease sale made while the new RMP is being drafted would prejudice the revision. Further, the protest letter notes that although a number of nearby lease sales are proposed, no attempt is made to assess their cumulative effect.

WELC attorney Kyle Tisdel repeatedly points out how the BLM's UFO proposed actions are violations of federal law—the National Environmental Policy Act (NEPA) and BLM's guiding statute, the Federal Land Policy Management Act (FLPMA)—in terms of public input, impact analysis, predetermined outcome and lack of an updated management plan. Not only does the BLM contend analysis is unnecessary before the permitting stage, it maintains that any problems that might arise can be "mitigated," thus rationalizing its finding of no significance. Quoting the BLM's Final Environmental Assessment: "To mitigate any potential impact that oil and gas development emissions may have on regional air quality, Best Management Practice (BMPs) may be required for any development project." But no attempt is made to determine what those potential impacts might be, whether they are risks worth taking, or how the "Best Management Practices" might solve the problems. Quoting from the Protest: "The agency is also presupposing that oil and gas resources, if developed, outweigh non-oil and gas resources, like wildlife habitat, air quality, water quality protection, as well as maintaining the socio-economic character of the

North Fork Valley," a noteworthy point, as a key purpose of NEPA is to ensure that environmental factors are weighted equally.

The protest letter shows the BLM's failure to analyze impacts to air quality, climate change, farmlands, land resources (soil, slopes, vegetation); seismicity, wildlife, water resources (ground water, surface water, wild and scenic rivers); transportation, recreation, visual resources and socio economics. And it states, "Given the magnitude of the proposed action and impacts to the communities of the North Fork Valley that this lease sale will create, BLM's FONSI is completely unsupportable."

The protest points out that the BLM includes no analysis on potential impacts from hydraulic fracturing itself, a technology not available at the time of the 1989 RMP; gives no attention to methane leaks or other greenhouse gas concerns; and does not address resiliency and the importance of the nation's farmland. In conclusion the protest states, "Any action taken that undermines a community's welfare and capacity to provide for itself in the face of recognized changes to climate—such as recklessly allowing for oil and gas development without even analyzing those impacts to farmland –is not only impermissible under NEPA, but also indefensible pursuant to BLM's mandate to act as stewards of our public lands."

The WELC protest letter arrives at the BLM in mid December, just two months before the date scheduled for lease sales. WELC announces, "To protect the communities' drinking and agricultural water supply, clean air, and thriving rural economy, we submitted a formal protest with the BLM Colorado State Office seeking removal of all public lands in the North Fork Valley scheduled to be sold in the February 2013 oil and gas lease sale. The BLM has 60 days to rule on our petition. If denied, we will go to court to stop this irresponsible gas fracking project."

Late January 2013, no word from BLM regarding WELC's official protest on behalf of CHC, and the proposed date for lease sales is just a couple weeks away. So it looks like hardball time. January 25, as CHC and WELC prepare for litigation, CHC sends a letter to state and federal BLM officials. CHC's E.D. Jim Ramey thanks BLM acting director Mike Pool and deputy director Neil Kornze for meeting with North Fork's coalition of residents in Washington D.C. He reminds them of the upcoming lease sale and the public's near unanimous concerns, particularly upsetting with the BLM working under the rubric of a Reagan-era Resource Management Plan and neither studying nor acknowledging current situations. CHC hopes that residents can continue to work with the BLM during the RMP revision and requests that the federal office, to the extent possible, take immediate action to "help facilitate a collaborative non-litigious process."

The letter goes on to express frustration that local BLM officials have discouraged public input at local town councils and have been unwilling to answer questions directly. Also disheartening has been the officials' apparent attempt to mislead and divide the community in inaccurate news releases. For the CHC, Jim Ramey concludes, "It is our sincere hope that litigation can be avoided and that BLM will work with North Fork Valley residents to prepare an RMP that reflects the present reality of this community… However, if litigation is the only option that we are afforded, our attorneys at the Western Environmental Law Center are prepared to file." Copies of the letter go also to U.S. senators and representatives, a state senator and representative, the Delta County commissioners and the Paonia town council.

And then miraculously, or so it seems to some of the onlookers, February 6, BLM defers all parcels. Colorado State BLM Director Helen Hankins says, "We've listened to concerns raised in numerous comments and public meetings. We are responding by deferring the North Fork Valley parcels at this time." Kyle Tisdel points to this as an example where organizing and legal strategy can come together to reach a successful resolution.

The BLM finally recognizes that their Resource Management Plan must be updated before it can rationally propose selling drilling leases. CHC's Jim Ramey is delighted that the BLM will be "slowing down and taking a closer look at the severe impacts of drilling."

Not surprisingly, industry groups don't share that delight. Kathleen Sgamma of the Western Energy Alliance argues that farming and gas drilling coexist in many places. Western Slope Colorado Oil and Gas Association Executive Director David Ludlam had already been annoyed that Ken Salazar, President Obama's Interior Secretary, requires proposed drilling parcels to be identified early, the BLM to conduct reviews, and that public input be sought. It just adds work and slows things down from the industry point of view. He says that the current decision takes a bad situation and makes it worse.

But much of the North Fork Valley is overjoyed. "This is what we wanted," says Mark Waltermire, "a chance to get the management plan to reflect the valley's promise."

Then on February 13, more good news: U.S. District Court Senior Judge Richard P. Matsch declares unlawful the BLM policy of concealing from the public the identities of those nominating public lands for resource extraction. Judge Matsch points out that knowing names makes bids competitive and competition elicits a fair price for publicly owned minerals. Additionally, the identity of the submitter can help concerned citizens evaluate the submitter's history of environmental stewardship.

The judge's decision is a big deal. For the first time since the oil and gas boom began, the public's right to know is affirmed. "A precedent has been set," Jim Ramey exults. "This is a victory for everyone who believes the government should do its business in the open." Though the FOIA case had specifically requested identification of the nominators in and around the North Fork Valley, the decision will affect BLM-managed public lands across the nation.

"Every community has a right to know what corporations are seeking to drill on public lands near their homes or where they recreate," said WELC's Kyle Tisdel.

While the community cheers that decision,

the committee of organic growers, vintners, ranchers, business people and conservationists working on the North Fork Alternative Plan puts on the finishing touches and gives it its public debut. Chaired by CHC's Jim Ramey and TCC's Sarah Sauter, the "community alternative" adapts existing BLM management tools to protect the North Fork's unique attributes, including prime wildlife habitat, delicate soils, domestic and irrigation water supplies; hunting, fishing, backpacking and other recreational areas; as well as tools to safeguard existing and emerging economies. The guiding philosophy is that even if oil and gas drilling must happen, it doesn't have to happen everywhere. Some places should be off the table. The multiple-use doctrine doesn't require destroying existing uses to favor the proposed use. And some things—water, air, children—are inviolate.

The public broadly supports the North Fork Alternative Plan but wonders if they dare hope the BLM will consider it. They've learned though, that it's counterproductive to try to second-guess the agency. The BLM has until Monday, April 15 to appeal Judge Matsch's decision that lease nominator identities must be made public. So far, there's been no word. However, with the valley's orchards in astonishing bloom, by mid-month BLM officials release what had, until now, been considered secret information. The nominators include Gunnison Energy, owned by Bill Koch and long associated with coal mining north of Paonia; Contex Energy Company of Denver; and by far the largest number of parcels, Denver's Baseline Minerals, Inc.

The only problem is that Contex and Baseline are industry land-men, companies that research, negotiate and bid on behalf of someone else, leaving still cloaked the identity of the company who would do the actual drilling. And although Kyle Tisdel and Jim Ramey laud both this precedent-setting decision and BLM'S cooperation in revealing names, the Bureau seems reluctant to revise their policy to reflect the Court order requiring real transparency. In May, twenty-nine organizations

will, with WELC's help, petition the BLM to update their policy.

Meanwhile CHC, with input from the scientists at Theo Colborn's The Endocrine Disruption Exchange (TEDX), launches a cutting-edge citizen-science air-quality sampling project. For a twenty-four hour period twice a month, with four sets a year, volunteers will wear backpacks equipped with air-sampling devices as they go about their daily routines.

When the industry gets complaints that oil and gas drilling pollutes the air and affects people's health, industry spokesmen sometimes argue that no one can prove the pollutants were not present before the drilling began, nor can they show that people actually breathe that particular air. This project speaks to both arguments. The backpack devices sample exactly the air the volunteer breathes, and through this project, a baseline of air quality can be established. CHC also is developing a handbook on their methods, to help other communities that wish to test for air quality. North Fork's first sampling is scheduled for September.

2013 continues in a sunny upbeat vein: In June, the Forest Service withdraws drilling approval in the Gunnison headwaters. July sees the 67th annual celebration of Paonia's Cherry Days. In September, volunteers begin donning backpacks, and air sampling commences. Then the valley celebrates its bounty in the Harvest Festival, with music, poetry, classes in sustainable living, sampling the valley's good food and wine, and dancing in the streets.

In October, the BLM agrees to consider the carefully crafted North Fork Alternative Plan as it revises the Resource Management Plan for the area. Happy day! Brent Helleckson, owner of Stone Cottage Cellars and representative of the West Elks Winery Association, notes that the Alternative Plan offers "reasonable recommendations to make sure we keep the North Fork the vibrant, beautiful, creative and agricultural hub that it is... (T)he North Fork plan would go a long way to protect

investments this community has already made."

AMBER KLEINMAN, a Paonia Town Council trustee points out that, "People don't move to Paonia to live in an industrial zone." The NFAP is a "sensible and prudent, resource-based approach to protecting what is important to the town and our residents—clean water, incredible scenery and a rural lifestyle."

Realtor Bob Lario adds, "The North Fork Plan is very protective of the valley's resources and character, and that in turn is good for attracting investment and new business and protecting property values."

Jim Ramey promises, "We will continue to work with the BLM to make sure that the agency adopts the alternative plan into the final Resource Management Plan."

"We live here because we love the land and the place," Thistle-Whistle owner and Valley Organic Growers Association president Mark Waltermire observes. "We need the clean water; we breathe the clean air. We want to raise our families in a farm field, not an oil field...(W)e are grateful and hopeful about this chance to make our voices heard. We love this place and will stand up for it."

Then 2014 explodes on the scene with the discovery that the Forest Service has approved BLM plans to drill as many as five wells in Gunnison National Forest, near Little Henderson Creek, in the headwaters of the North Fork of the Gunnison River. Each well pad requires approximately ten acres and affects many more with parking lots, other activity areas and required spacing between wells, plus hundreds of miles of access roads. Mark Waltermire points out that each well demands up to a thousand truck trips carrying fracking fluid chemicals and heavy equipment. "If there's a big spill, or one of those trucks crashes and contaminates the ditch water we rely on, we would pay the price. We can't risk our water supply."

Federal law requires the Forest Service to analyze possible impacts before approval, which they failed to do. July 28, WELC files suit on behalf of Citizens for a Healthy Community (CHC) and High Country Conservation Advocates. August 7 brings a Forest Service letter agreeing to withdraw drilling permits in the Gunnison headwaters. The Forest Service and the BLM will together conduct a comprehensive environmental analysis that they will make public before proceeding.

More good news comes toward the end of the year when the Forest Service closes large swaths of the Thompson Divide to further leasing and adds protections to roadless areas. The Divide's Wilderness Workshop and the Thompson Divide Coalition still hope for legislative action to withdraw the entire Divide from future leasing and to buy out or negotiate trades for existing leases.

Such progress cannot come too soon. On November 14 Theo Colborn stuns the valley populace with the urgency of an essay stressing how ubiquitous fossil gasses are, including the many aromatics, semi-gaseous liquids that escape from well heads. She correlates increased human exposure through the past fifty years to a similar increase in hormone-driven cancers, infertility, neurological disorders and a host of other effects. Even in minute quantities, these hormone-mimicking gases act on cell development from egg to senescence, affecting the structure, function, intelligence and behavior of the individual. She points out that aromatics near well heads have been found at more than three times the concentration known to cause birth defects. She reminds her readers that scientists know humans are causing climate change through the use of fossil fuels, but ends her essay saying that endocrine disruption is a far more imminent threat. Governments must act quickly, she says, "or too few healthy, intelligent people will remain to preserve a humanitarian society and create some semblance of world peace."

A month later, at age 87, Dr. Colborn is dead from lung damage that she blamed on exposure to cadmium, a toxic mineral she contacted in her sampling of Colorado streams some thirty years earlier. Though she will be sorely missed, her research, her writings, her courage and her resolve will continue to inspire. Under the guidance of **DR. CAROL KWIATKOWSKI,** The Endocrine Disruption Exchange will continue her work.

April 2015, SG Interests and Ursa, two gas companies with more than 40,000 acres of leases in the Thompson Divide, propose trading that land for leases in Garfield and Delta Counties. Some see a relief for the Divide but Peter Hart, Wilderness Workshop attorney, notes that the proposal includes no protection for the area of vacated leases, which were illegal in the first place. Why should the lease owners get another ten years to destroy somewhere else?

Fortunately energy concerns need not always be negative. Early May, Pete Kolbenschlag presents a three-day Climate Challenge and Solar Fair hosted by Climate Colorado and **Solar Energy International (SEI)**.

Founded in 1991, SEI is a nonprofit educational organization headquartered in Paonia that provides technical training in renewable energy and sustainable practices to empower people, communities and businesses worldwide. They give hands-on workshops and online courses in solar photovoltaics, micro-hydro and solar hot water technology, working throughout the Americas as well as in Africa, Micronesia and the Caribbean. Climate Colorado challenges communities to find ways to reduce individual and community carbon footprints to net zero and water consumption to half. "We can't wait for the political system to respond," Pete says, "especially when Colorado loses. We are positioned to be global leaders."

September brings big changes to the Valley's conservation groups. Sarah Sauter, who has been an organizational dynamo for The Conservation Center, accepts the position of Program Manager for Oregon's Rogue River Watershed Council. But TCC is not left empty-handed. That Vista intern who had left 500 local residents

spellbound with his Google-earth virtual fly-over of the valley at the first public meeting about the BLM's lease plans back in January 2012—that was Alex Johnson. And now **ALEX JOHNSON** takes over the reins of The Western Slope Conservation Center.

Two months later another Valley star is recognized when The Wilderness Society, a leading national conservation organization, hires away CHC Executive Director Jim Ramey, to be the new outreach coordinator for its energy and climate campaign. But here also, the conservation cooperative is not left flat-footed. Board member and international trade attorney **NATASHA LÉGER** agrees to give her considerable talents to CHC as interim ED.

The West Slope gets an early Christmas present on December 16 of 2015 when the BLM proposes cancelling leases in the White River National Forest. If they are cancelled, none will be exchanged. But the following June, the BLM releases the long-awaited draft of the RMP revision and although the North Fork Alternative is included, the agency's preferred alternative largely maintains the status quo of fossil fuel exploitation. The Uncompahgre district manages more than 650,000 acres of surface area plus another 971,220 subsurface areas of federal mineral estate. Their preferred plan proposes to open 95 percent of the BLM lands and minerals to oil and gas leasing.

CHC and other groups, residents, and the County request an extension of the comment period on the draft RMP. BLM grants a sixty-day extension, to November 1. On that date, on behalf of CHC, Center for Biological Diversity, Earthjustice, Sierra Club, WildEarth Guardians, and Wilderness Workshop, WELC files extensive comments. They request inclusion of a "no leasing alternative" on the basis of (1) incompatibility between fossil fuels and North Fork's other incomparable resources, and (2) that current climate science and carbon budgeting demand a different set of priorities on public lands, stressing that we must keep fossil fuel resources in the ground if we hope to maintain a livable planet. By the November 1 deadline the UFO field office has received an unprecedented 53,000 comments, including more than 42,000 recommending a No

Leasing alternative. BLM's final RMP is scheduled for fall of 2018.

July 2016, Pete Kolbenschlag and a delegation from Colorado Farm and Food Alliance, the Western Slope Conservation Center, and Solar Energy International visit offices of both Colorado senators, the EPA, BLM, and the White House Council on Environmental Quality to bring the message that with orchards and coal growing up together, and together powering the economy of the North Fork Valley, that heritage can transition to the 21st century with development of clean and sustainable energy. Besides the West Slope's tremendous solar potential, streams and canals that drop into the valley from high in the Rockies can power small and medium-scale hydro projects, and methane emitted from even shuttered mines can be (and is being) captured to generate electricity. It is important, one delegate says, that the officials and agencies understand that solutions are available right now to boost the economy, create jobs and protect the valley without contributing further to climate change.

November 9, 2016, Donald Trump, who denies the fact of climate change and apparently declares allegiance to the oil and gas companies, is elected President of the United States.

One week later, Interior Secretary Sally Jewel, BLM Director Neil Kornze and Governor Hickenlooper meet at the Colorado Capitol to announce the cancellation of 25 undeveloped oil and gas leases in the Thompson Divide, after the BLM acknowledged deficiencies in the original analysis of 65 leases in the area. Jewell declares the decision "a testament to the ability of individuals, businesses, governments and organizations in Colorado to work together to find solutions…for the local community, economy and environment."

But industry representatives call it a "taking" and contend that the decision came about because in its waning days, the Obama administration is doing the bidding of environmental groups. SG Interest's Robbie Guinn and industry representatives say they will look for relief in the courts and expect the new Republican administration to uphold the old lease contracts.

Carbondale-based Thompson Divide Coalition argues that rather than being political, the decision is a response to over 50,000 comments from local citizens and governments and those who work and recreate in the beautiful Thompson Divide.

January 20, 2017, Donald J. Trump is inaugurated as the 45th president of the United States. Almost immediately, all mention of climate change disappears from the White House website. President Obama's Climate Action Plan, which proposes to cut carbon pollution, prepare for the effects of climate change and lead international efforts in addressing climate issues is replaced by the incoming administration's America First Energy Plan. "America First" calls for eliminating "burdensome regulations" that discourage development.

The U.S. Department of Agriculture and Environmental Protection Agency (EPA) employees are instructed not to communicate with the public. The EPA is ordered to remove its Climate Change web pages, but the next day that order is rescinded. Though the order was rescinded, the climate page did eventually come down, and scientific information considered politically inconvenient is constantly buried or deleted.

Under the obscure Congressional Revision Act, which fast-tracks congressional ability to overturn rules without public input, Congress kills a rule restricting the dumping of toxic mining waste into streams. This rule primarily affects mining practices associated with mountaintop removal. Appalachian Voices says that coal companies have buried over 2000 miles of streams since the 1990s, with heavy-metal waste polluting water sources and causing widespread and serious health effects.

Another bill moves forward to overturn the BLM methane and waste-prevention rule via the Congressional Review Act. The America First Energy Plan states that the Trump administration "will embrace the shale and gas revolution to bring jobs and prosperity to millions of Americans." The bill fails initially, but the BLM is reviewing the rule pursuant to Trump's Executive Orders, and suspends compliance deadlines. A short time later, Ruth Welch, BLM State Director, along with State Directors from Alaska and New Mexico, are reassigned to non-BLM agencies, presumably for being progressive on the environment and potentially problematic to Trump's America-first energy vision.

At the time of this writing, the Trump Administration continues its rollbacks of environmental regulations and protections putting public health, safety and the environment at risk and climate change adaptation in flux. Valley farmers are already feeling the effects of climate change, with earlier bud-break, warmer summers and falls, more erratic weather, more agricultural pests, but most importantly, changes in the watershed. The North Fork Valley gets very little rainfall, most of its domestic and irrigation water coming from snowmelt. Less snow is falling now and it's melting sooner. Some aspen groves are dying, with loss not only of their beauty and ecosystem communities, but also their shading of streams, exacerbating earlier snowmelt. If irrigation ditches run out of water in August, farms and ranches could be devastated.

Coloradoans tell stories of water sources poisoned by fracking. A single fracked well can take as much as eight million gallons of water. The methane transported, flared, and leaking from wellheads is a greenhouse gas many times more potent than carbon dioxide in its potential to cause global warming. Rural gas gathering pipelines are unregulated so there is no way of the public knowing if there are any incremental failures along those pipelines, yet, government and industry say "nothing to worry about." For the planet, for the climate, for the vineyards and farms and ranches, for the artists and the tourists, for the people, for the children, the North Fork Valley will look for a no-fracking alternative.

Citizens for a Healthy Community, High Country Conservation Advocates, Western Environmental Law Center, Earthjustice, The Wilderness Society and so many more are energized and determined. As famously said by Margaret Mead, "Never doubt that a small group of thoughtful, committed citizens can change the world. Indeed, it is the only thing that ever has."

Author Bio:

Gardener, one-time nursery owner and teacher, grateful great grandmother, perennial star gazer and admirer of the alchemy of sun rays on the treemoss, Evelyn Searle Hess is spending the winter chapter of her life writing books. Her *To the Woods: Sinking Roots, Living Lightly and Finding True Home,* OSU Press 2010, recounts the revelations, joys and challenges during fifteen years that Hess and her husband David lived without electricity or indoor  plumbing on their wooded property in the foothills southwest of Eugene, Oregon. It celebrates wild nature through the seasons while it explores relationships with and within the natural world, with fellow humans throughout the world and with each other.

Hess's second book, *Building a Better Nest,* OSU Press 2015, explores the paths and roadblocks to living a sustainable life. It looks at what a house can do, resilience in gardening and putting up food, ways to relate to the ecosystem and its species and problems with consumerism and the economy's growth model. It finds hope in lessons from ancestors, in family and in community and looks to a new model. Now Hess is researching people-power—stories of people working together for the betterment of the planet and each other.

Hess's book *To the Woods,* won the WILLA award for best creative non-fiction of 2010. Her *Building a Better Nest* was named one of the best books of 2015 by Multnomah Libraries, and made the short list for best Indie Environmental Non-fiction.

Addendum

People of the North Fork Valley honor two important values: the call of citizenship, and that of morality. May we all follow their lead.

This nation's government was founded of, by, and for the people according to Abraham Lincoln. Nowhere can I find a suggestion that it was to be of, by or for corporations, or for maximizing the profits of the few. As citizens of a democracy, we have the right, and I would say the responsibility, to inform ourselves and speak out regarding decisions affecting our health or welfare.

The moral angle is equally potent. Whether moved by the biblical exhortation to protect God's creation or by the knowledge that breathable air, potable water, fertile soil and a livable climate are essential for ourselves and for future generations, deep-felt morality requires us to protect this verdant planet.

Government bureaus are supported by taxpayers: We the people pay the bills. It is reasonable for us to understand and give input about what we are paying for.

Relevant government agencies regarding extraction of our federal public minerals or oil and gas activity on split-estates (where surface and mineral rights are severed and one or the other is owned by the federal government (the public) or private property owners) include:

- Bureau of Land Management | https://www.blm.gov
  - *For the North Fork Valley specifically*
    https://www.blm.gov/contact/colorado
    - Uncompahgre Field Office
    - Colorado River Valley Field Office
      (Oil and gas activity in the North Fork Valley was consolidated under the CRVFO in 2015)
    - Colorado State Office

- US Forest Service | https://www.fs.usda.gov
  - *For the North Fork Valley specifically*
    - Grand Mesa Uncompahgre and Gunnison National Forests
      https://www.fs.usda.gov/gmug
    - White River National Forest
      https://www.fs.usda.gov/whiteriver

- Colorado State Agencies
  - *Colorado Oil and Gas Conservation Commission*
    https://cogcc.state.co.us
  - *Colorado Department of Public Health and Environment*
    https://www.colorado.gov/cdphe

Each citizen's voice is crucial. A chorus of voices carries farther and wider. The following groups were on the pages of *Frack War*. Many more groups than these are doing good work. To join a chorus, or for information, or to give support, check out these websites or others.

Appalachian Voices | appvoices.org

Center for Biological Diversity | https://biologicaldiversity.org

Citizens for a Healthy Community (CHC) | www.chc4you.org

Climate Colorado—Switch 2020 | climatecolorado.org

Colorado Farm and Food Alliance | www.coloradofarmfood.org

Earthjustice | https://earthjustice.org

High Country Conservation Advocates | https://www.hccacb.org

Mountain West Strategies | mountainweststrategies.com

Sierra Club | https://www.sierraclub.org

Solar Energy International | https://www.solarenergy.org

The Endocrine Disruption Exchange (TEDX) |
    https://endocrinedisruption.org

Valley Organic Growers Association | http://vogaco.org

Western Environmental Law Center (WELC) | https://westernlaw.org

Western Slope Conservation Center aka The Conservation Center
    (TCC) | westernslopeconservation.org

Wild Earth Guardians | https://wildearthguardians.org

Wilderness Workshop | wildernessworkshop.org

In Solidarity,
Evelyn Searle Hess
July 2018

CPSIA information can be obtained
at www.ICGtesting.com
Printed in the USA
BVHW040604290119
538842BV00037B/5064/P